I See . . . A Lot of Weeds

Written by Mary Barth
Illustrations and Photographs by Richard Barth

Gotham Books

30 N Gould St.
Ste. 20820, Sheridan, WY 82801
https://gothambooksinc.com/

Phone: 1 (307) 464-7800

© 2024 *Mary Barth*. All rights reserved.

No part of this book may be reproduced, stored in a retrieval system, or transmitted by any means without the written permission of the author.

Published by Gotham Books (June 7, 2024)

ISBN: 979-8-3302-2119-6 (P)
ISBN: 979-8-3302-2120-2 (E)

Because of the dynamic nature of the Internet, any web addresses or links contained in this book may have changed since publication and may no longer be valid.

The views expressed in this work are solely those of the author and do not necessarily reflect the views of the publisher, and the publisher hereby disclaims any responsibility for them.

This book is dedicated to our wonderful daughter, Nicole, who strives every day to protect our environment and our beautiful and adventureous grandchildren, Kamari and Judah.

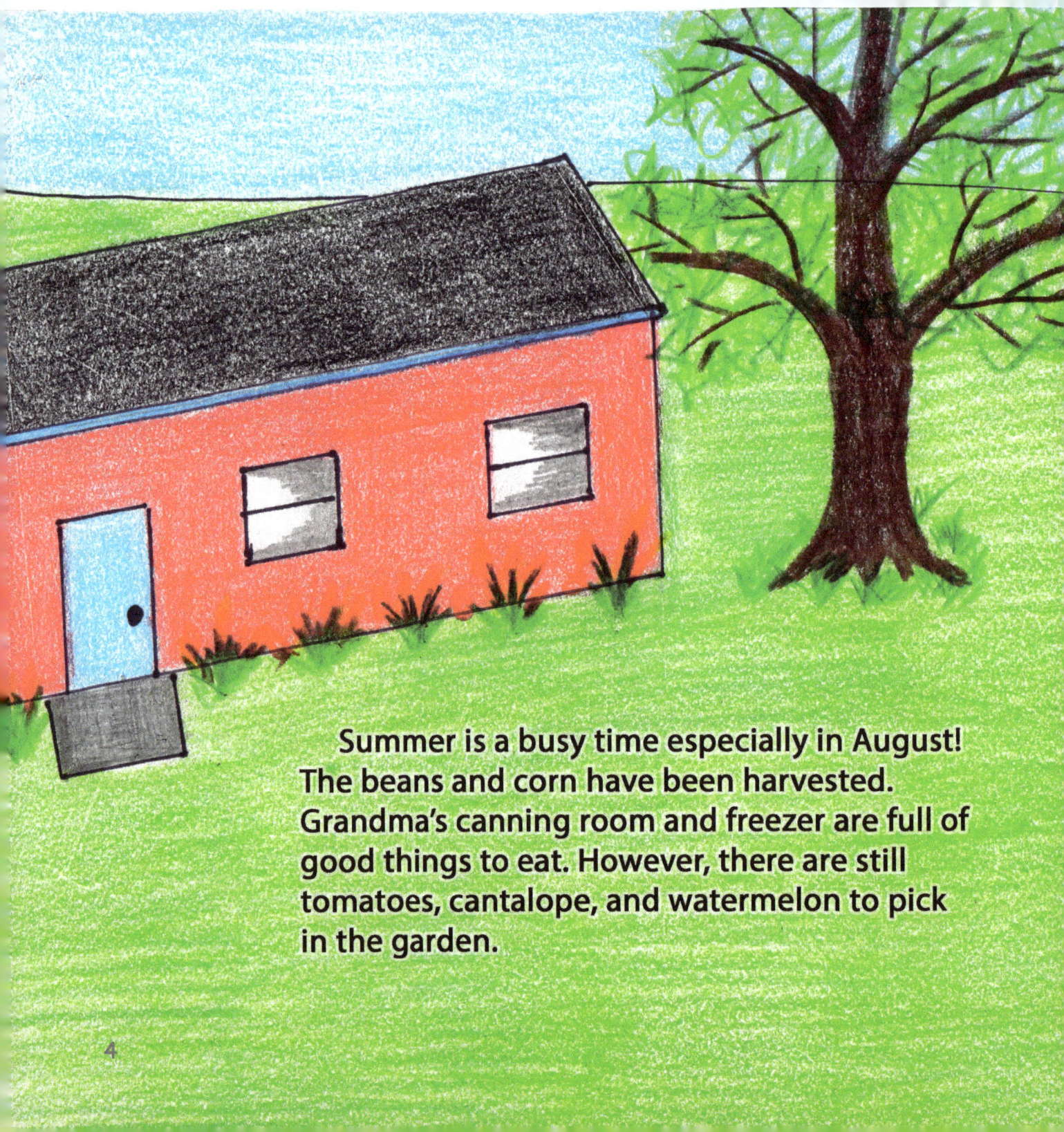

Summer is a busy time especially in August! The beans and corn have been harvested. Grandma's canning room and freezer are full of good things to eat. However, there are still tomatoes, cantalope, and watermelon to pick in the garden.

Grandma says she hates weeds, but I know differently. Yesterday when I came to help pick tomatoes, Grandpap was mowing. He was doing something really strange--he was mowing around some weeds!

This special weed--called the milkweed-- is Grandma's favorite weed! Wait a minute, I thought she hated weeds!

Grandpap says that milkweed grows all over - meadows, gardens, farmers' fields, and even along the highways.

The milkweed's leaves are food for many insects, and its flowers are nectar for other insects such as bees and butterflies. However, for the larvae of monarch butterflies, milkweed bugs, and milkweed leaf beetles, this plant is their only food. Without the milkweed they cannot survive.

"Look! She is laying an egg!
Let's keep this happening."

Last year I did a report on the monarch butterfly for school. I found out a lot of facts about this beautiful butterfly and the plant it depends on. For example, milkweed plants grow in families. They send out their roots and small milkweed plants pop up and grow in the same area--families. In the fall this butterfly migrates, or flies south, to winter with many other monarchs. More importantly, however, these wonderful creatures are beginning to disappear!

The monarch is my favorite butterfly because of its bright orange and black colors. Every August I find lots of caterpillars on the milkweed around my Grandparents' yard that I can watch hatch into the beautiful butterflies.

Since school will be starting soon, we head to the outlet stores. You can get sneakers, clothes, toys, and games for a lower cost. I like the restaurants too! There are places to get burgers, hot dogs, pizza, and even salads!

As we drive, I see a small family of milkweed by the side of the road and wonder how many caterpillars might be eating their way to becoming a butterfly right now!

Then I see it--a large tractor pulling a mower is cutting the grass in the strip between the four lanes of highway. Mowing the grass is one thing, but stripping all the milkweed plants of their leaves is another!

I feel like I have butterflies in my stomach-- what can I do? I want to save the milkweed and the caterpillars that may be on them.

Maybe I can do what they did at a state park about two hours from our house. The staff at this park placed signs along the road by each family of milkweed plants so the plants can be identified and protected from being cut down.

I know that some farmers are spraying this weed to keep it out of their crops and that houses are being built where milkweed once stood.

Many places are flooding and with our changing climate there is a lot of severe hot and cold weather. Wow, no wonder it is difficult for the milkweed to thrive!

What can I do to save the milkweed plant and, with it, the monarch butterfly?

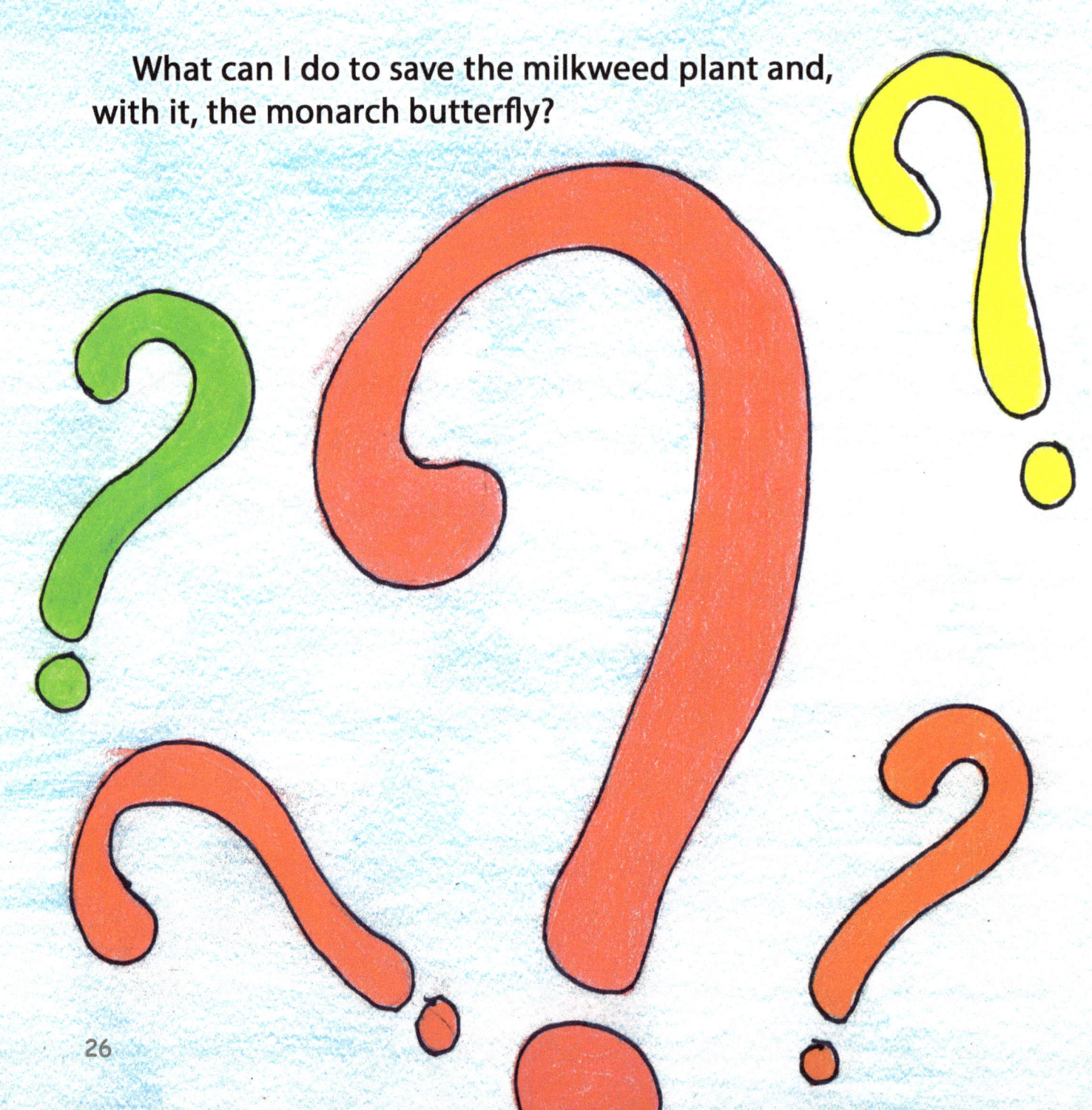

When I get home I'm calling Grandma to see if she knows who is in charge of the mowing along our road, but for now I'm going to save some milkweed seeds and plant them, care for them, and protect them. I want this beautiful butterfly to survive! Maybe if I tell enough people they will help me too!

www.ingramcontent.com/pod-product-compliance
Lightning Source LLC
LaVergne TN
LVHW072130060526
838201LV00071B/5007